# PAINTE FURNITURE

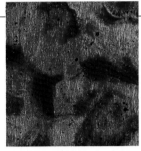

In your hands, timeworn furniture can be born again, using your favorite crafting techniques — painting, decoupage, stenciling, stamping, marbling, and more! Now those relics that were destined for the dumpster can be transformed into shining showpieces you might expect to find in the window of a custom craft shop or wearing a blue ribbon at the state fair!

Half the fun, of course, is going treasure hunting to find these fine old restorable pieces. You can search your favorite flea markets, stop at a few yard sales, visit second-hand stores, or discover forgotten treasures in your attic or garage! You could even start with unfinished furniture purchased from a local store.

Along the way, you'll craft with complete confidence by following our straightforward, step-by-step instructions. Every project is shown in full-color photographs so you can see the end result before you start. Even beginners will be able to stand back and proudly show off their beautifully restored masterpieces!

Say "no" to sky-high decorator prices as you relax and enjoy fashioning unique functional furniture pieces from surprising sources — at a fraction of the cost. Let your imagination run wild as you personalize your work with your color combinations, patterns, and one-of-a-kind embellishments. Enjoy your adventure!

LEISURE ARTS, INC.
Little Rock, Arkansas

# CONTENTS

## tables and chairs

## cabinets

# leopard-print coffee table

*C*reate this wildly luxurious look with random spots of paint and gold highlights.

**You will need** a wooden coffee table; yellow, purple, brown, black, and metallic gold acrylic paints; maple stain; gold buffing cream; soft cotton cloth; paintbrushes; primer; sealer; and any additional supplies from Step 1.

1. Read Painting Materials, Preparing Project, Masking, Painting Project, Antiquing, and Sealing Project, page 73.

2. Prepare table for painting. Paint tabletop yellow. Paint remainder of table purple.

3. Refer to photo, page 37, to paint random spots on tabletop using brown and black.

Continued on pg. 37

# poster-topped accent table

Stain and top an end table with an appealing poster devoted to your favorite subject.

**You will need** a wooden end table; a poster the same size or slightly larger than tabletop; oak stain; sponge brush; spray adhesive; sealer; glass top cut to fit tabletop; and any additional supplies from Step 1.

1. Read Painting Materials, Preparing Project, Staining Project, and Sealing Project, page 73.

2. Prepare table for staining. Stain table.

3. Cut the poster to fit dimensions of tabletop minus $1/4$" on all sides. Use spray adhesive to adhere poster to tabletop.

4. Apply three coats of sealer to table.

5. Place glass top on table.

# technique sampler sofa table

$m$ask off your tabletop into equal squares to sample our assortment of faux finishes.

**You will need** a wooden sofa table; honey maple gel stain; yardstick; dark green, green, light green, yellow green, white, antique gold, metallic gold, burnt umber, bronze, and black acrylic paints; mop brush; flat brush; paintbrushes; striping tool; glazing medium; combing tool; isopropyl alcohol; eyedropper; plastic wrap; natural sponge; soft cotton cloth; feather; primer; matte sealer; and any additional supplies from Step 1.

1. Read Painting Materials, Preparing Project, Masking, Painting Project, Staining Project, Painting Basics, Burled Wood, Fossilizing, Malachite, Marbling, Sponging, Tiger Eye Maple, Tortoise Shell, and Sealing Project, page 73.

2. Prepare table for staining. Mask off a rectangle 1" inside edges of tabletop. Remove drawers. Following manufacturer's instructions, stain table outside masked off area. Remove tape.

Continued on pg. 37

# refined accent table

Paint a little table with classic shapes on top and highlight the raised areas with rub-on gold. Age the table with crackle medium and antique gel.

**You will need** a round wooden table; black, antique gold, brown, gold, and metallic gold acrylic paints; gold buffing cream; Jo Sonja's® crackle medium; black water-based antique gel; paintbrushes; soft cotton cloth; primer; sealer; and any additional supplies from Step 1.

1. Read Painting Materials, Preparing Project, Painting Project, Transferring Patterns, Painting Basics, Antiquing, Crackling, and Sealing Project, page 73.

2. Prepare table for painting. Paint table black.

Continued on pg. 37

# chinoiserie table

Use gesso to create textured mountains, temples, and other elements of Chinese scenery on this traditional table.

**You will need** a wooden coffee table; black, metallic gold, and metallic silver acrylic paints; gesso; toothpicks; #10/0 liner brush; paintbrushes; primer; sealer; and any additional supplies from Step 1.

1. Read Painting Materials, Preparing Project, Masking, Painting Project, Painting Basics, and Sealing Project, page 73.

2. Prepare table for painting. Paint table black.

3. For border design, mask off 2" from edges of table. Paint thin outer border, edges of table, and thin inner border metallic gold. Referring to photo, pages 50 and 51, use a pencil to lightly mark diagonal lines 1" apart between border lines. Use water to thin metallic gold and metallic silver paints to ink-like consistencies. Paint border detail lines with thinned paints. Add undiluted metallic silver dip dots to intersections.

4. Refer to photo and use toothpick to apply gesso to table to create raised volcano, trees, boats, and outlines of pagodas; let dry. Apply a second coat of gesso to build up designs. Paint designs black.

Continued on pg. 38

# work-of-art table

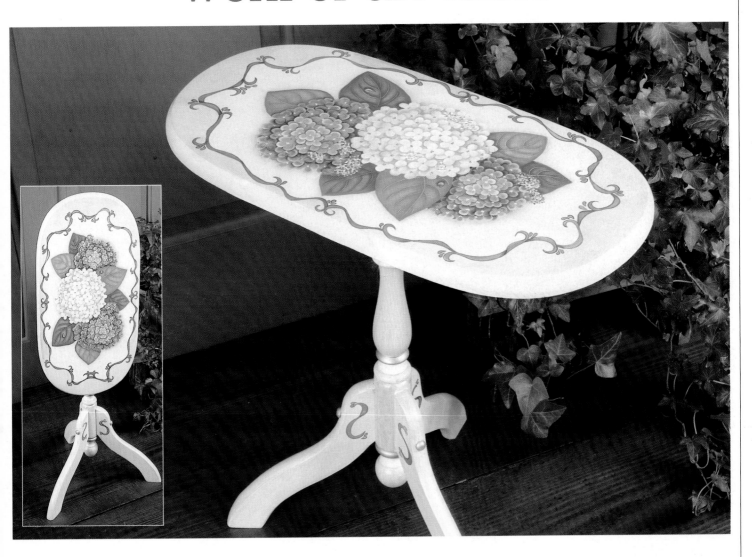

turn a tiny tabletop into a work of art with our floral design. Color-wash the edges and legs.

**You will need** a wooden tilt-top table; white, off-white, light purple, antique white, light green, green, dark green, purple, blue, violet, black, and metallic silver acrylic paints; small liner brush; paintbrushes; primer; sealer; and any additional supplies from Step 1.

1. Read Painting Materials, Preparing Project, Painting Project, Transferring Patterns, Painting Basics, and Sealing Project, page 73.

2. Prepare table for painting. Paint table off-white.

3. Transfer outer edges of flower and leaf photo pattern, pages 52 and 53, to tabletop. Basecoat purple flowers with light purple and the white flower with antique white. Basecoat three leaves with light green and three remaining leaves with green.

Continued on pg. 38

# painted lace accent table

$\mathcal{P}$aint a pattern of dots, comma strokes, and crisscross lines to create this lacy "doily." Highlight with a handpainted rose.

**You will need** a round wooden table; dark oak stain (optional); sanding sponge; white, pink, green, dark green, dark pink, very dark pink, light pink, very dark green, and light green acrylic paints; large flat brush; mop brush; liner brush; small round brush; paintbrushes; sealer; and any additional supplies from Step 1.

1. Read Painting Materials, Preparing Project, Staining Project, Transferring Patterns, Painting Basics, and Sealing Project, page 73.

Continued on pg. 38

# fern-stamped coffee table

I oll paint onto fresh ferns to make natural stamps for this pretty coffee table.

**You will need** a wooden coffee table; off-white, green, and dark green acrylic paints; light green, green, and dark green artist's oil paints; mineral spirits; paintbrushes; palette knife; piece of glass; brayer with hard rubber roller; paper or newsprint; paper towels; 15 to 20 fresh fern fronds; heavy book; primer; sealer; and any additional supplies from Step 1.

1. Read Painting Materials, Preparing Project, Masking, Painting Project, and Sealing Project, page 73.

2. Prepare table for painting. Paint table off-white.

3. Mask off a wide border around table top. Paint border with green acrylic paint. Mask off a narrow border along inner edge of wide border. Paint narrow border with dark green acrylic paint.

4. To flatten fronds, press fronds in book no longer than an hour as they will begin to wilt. After pressing, lay fronds on table for placement.

5. Squeeze oil paints onto glass; thin each color with mineral spirits to an ink-like consistency. Slightly mix colors as you roll brayer through thinned paints, spreading a thin layer evenly over roller.

Continued on pg. 39

# elegant-finish dining set

α*dd elegance to a classic dining table and chairs with burled wood and tortoise shell faux finishes.*

**You will need** a wooden dining room table and chairs with removable seats; yardstick; antique gold, metallic gold, brown, dark brown, burnt umber, bronze, and black acrylic paints; glazing medium; $^1/_8$"w, $1^1/_2$"w, and 2"w painter's masking tape; craft knife; isopropyl alcohol; eyedropper; paintbrushes; natural sponge; gold buffing cream; soft cotton cloth; primer; sealer; fabric for seats; batting; staple gun; and any additional supplies from Step 1.

1. Read Painting Materials, Preparing Project, Masking, Painting Project, Transferring Patterns, Painting Basics, Burled Wood, Tortoise Shell, Sealing Project, and Covering a Seat, page 73.

2. Prepare table for painting. Paint table support and desired portions of legs black. Paint remaining table parts antique gold.

3. Transfer medallion photo pattern, page 55, to center of tabletop, placing pattern so that when one of the lines crossing the center point is extended, it divides the table in half from side to side. Use a pencil and a yardstick to extend all lines from the center point to the table edge. Paint medallion metallic gold.

Continued on pg. 39

# fabulous '50s kitchen chairs

handpaint these chairs with cherries and plaid patterns from 1950s-vintage tablecloths.

**You will need** four wooden chairs with removable seats; matte white acrylic latex wall paint; red, dark red, green, blue, yellow, and white acrylic paints; #4 and #5/0 script liner brushes; paintbrushes; primer; sealer; red, blue, and yellow plaid and fruit motif fabric for seats; batting; staple gun; and any additional supplies from Step 1.

1. Read Painting Materials, Preparing Project, Masking, Painting Project, Transferring Patterns, Painting Basics, Sealing Project, and Covering a Seat, page 73.

2. Prepare chairs for painting. Paint chairs with white wall paint.

Continued on pg. 40

# kaleidoscope chair

$l$et your creativity run wild with a vivid medley of free-form color patterns.

**You will need** a wooden chair with removable seat; green, dark green, pink, yellow, white, and orange acrylic paints; paintbrushes; natural sponge; black medium-point permanent marker; primer; sealer; fabric for seat; batting; staple gun; and any additional supplies from Step 1.

1. Read Painting Materials, Preparing Project, Masking, Painting Project, Sponging, Sealing Project, and Covering a Seat, page 73.

2. Prepare chair for painting. Referring to photo for color placement and masking areas as necessary, paint chair green, pink, yellow, orange, and white.

Continued on pg. 40

14

# olde roses chair

Paint a bouquet of roses on an old-fashioned chair and highlight with metallic gold detail.

**You will need** a wooden chair with removable seat; ivory, white, light green, green, dark green, dark pink, blue, yellow, gold, and metallic gold acrylic paints; flat brushes; stiff-bristled brush; liner brush; paintbrushes; natural sponge; primer; sealer; fabric for seat; batting; staple gun; and any additional supplies from Step 1.

1. Read Painting Materials, Preparing Project, Painting Project, Transferring Patterns, Painting Basics, Sponging, Sealing Project, and Covering a Seat, page 73.

2. Prepare chair for painting. Paint chair ivory.

Continued on pg. 40

# crackle-finish stenciled armoire

*Choose dark brown paint for the undercoat and stenciling on this crackled armoire.*

**You will need** a wooden armoire, semi-gloss dark brown and matte beige latex enamel wall paints, matte cream acrylic latex wall paint, metallic gold acrylic paint, burnt umber oil paint, crackle medium (quart-size), roller, soft household paintbrush, paintbrushes, primer, sealer, and any additional supplies from Step 1.

1. Read Painting Materials, Preparing Project, Painting Project, Transferring Patterns, Painting Basics, Antiquing, Crackling, Stenciling, and Sealing Project, page 73.

2. Prepare armoire for painting. Use a roller to paint inside and outside of armoire with dark brown wall paint.

Continued on pg. 41

# fanciful hutch

**C**ombine *easy craft painting with stamping, stippling, and crackling to dress up this versatile hutch.*

**You will need** a wooden hutch; matte white and light blue acrylic latex wall paints; white, navy blue, light green, green, dark green, yellow, light gray, and brown acrylic paints; crackle medium (quart-size); stipple brush; #1 script liner brush; #10/0 liner brush; round brush; flat brush; paintbrushes; natural sponge; craft foam; craft glue; primer; sealer; and any additional supplies from Step 1.

1. Read Painting Materials, Preparing Project, Painting Project, Transferring Patterns, Painting Basics, Crackling, Sponging, and Sealing Project, page 73.

2. Prepare hutch for painting. Paint beaded paneling with white wall paint. Paint remainder of hutch with light blue wall paint.

Continued on pg. 41

# nautical-poster cabinet

Post a stunning sea scene over the sliding doors of a cabinet painted with nautical stripes and a mariner's compass.

**You will need** a wooden cabinet with sliding doors; white and dark blue acrylic paints; glazing medium; paintbrushes; spray adhesive; brayer; poster slightly larger than sliding doors of cabinet; craft knife; 2"w painter's masking tape; primer; sealer; and any additional supplies from Step 1.

1. Read Painting Materials, Preparing Project, Masking, Painting Project, Transferring Patterns, Painting Basics, Striping, and Sealing Project, page 73.

2. Prepare cabinet for painting. Paint cabinet white.

Continued on pg. 41

# pie safe with embossed insets

rescue *this old pie safe using our distressed paint technique and embossed wallpaper insets. Update the inside with fresh paper and fabric.*

**You will need** a wooden pie safe, desired paint or stain for underlying color (optional), wood trim for drawers, wood glue, matte antique white acrylic latex wall paint, rusty brown acrylic paint, paintbrushes, electric sander or sanding block with medium-grit sandpaper, embossed wallpaper for pressed tin look, wallpaper for lining shelves, cardboard, spray adhesive, household cement, fabric for lining inside of doors, paper-backed fusible web, mat board, painter's masking tape, sealer, and any additional supplies from Step 1.

1. Read Painting Materials, Preparing Project, Painting Project, Staining Project, Distressing, and Sealing Project, page 73.

Continued on pg. 42

# color-washed cabinet

g*o for the soft look on this little countertop cabinet with color-washed roses.*

**You will need** a wooden cabinet; yellow, rose, white, green, and blue acrylic paints; Jo Sonja's® crackle medium; paintbrushes; hair dryer; primer; sealer; and any additional supplies from Step 1.

1. Read Painting Materials, Preparing Project, Painting Project, Transferring Patterns, Painting Basics, Crackling, and Sealing Project, page 73.

2. Prepare cabinet for painting. Paint cabinet yellow.

3. Following manufacturer's instructions, apply crackle medium to cabinet. Use a hair dryer to help crackle medium process.

4. Transfer photo patterns, page 63, to cabinet front and sides, reversing patterns as needed.

Continued on pg. 42

# sunny gingham-look cupboard

**m**asking makes it easy to create this gingham look. Accent with handpainted details, then add years of "wear" by sanding the edges.

**You will need** a wooden cupboard; matte white acrylic latex wall paint; white, yellow, fuchsia, green, and blue acrylic paints; flat brush; paintbrushes; 1"w painter's masking tape; electric sander or sanding block with medium-grit sandpaper; sealer; and any additional supplies from Step 1.

1. Read Painting Materials, Preparing Project, Masking, Painting Project, Transferring Patterns, Painting Basics, Distressing, Striping, and Sealing Project, page 73.

2. Prepare cupboard for painting. Paint cupboard with two coats of white wall paint. Mask off 3"w stripes on inside cupboard back. Paint every other stripe with equal parts of white and yellow acrylic paints.

3. To achieve gingham effect, create vertical stripes of equal width using 1"w tape. Paint every other stripe with equal parts of white and yellow. Remove tape. Repeat, masking in opposite direction.

4. Transfer rose photo patterns, page 64, to top of cupboard, doors, knobs, and sides of cupboard. Paint roses with flat brush double-loaded with fuchsia and white.

5. Follow the contours of your cupboard to paint vines and leaves with green paint. Mix equal parts of white and yellow to paint veins and highlights on leaves.

6. Transfer rope photo pattern, page 64, to cupboard. Paint rope with flat brush double-loaded with blue and white.

7. For an aged effect, sand along edges of doors, openings, and knobs.

8. Apply sealer to cupboard.

# rustic chest with combing

**U**se glazing medium and a combing tool to create dramatic highlights on the top, side panels, and drawer fronts.

**You will need** a stained wooden chest, brown and tan acrylic paints, glazing medium, paintbrushes, combing tool, primer, sealer, and any additional supplies from Step 1.

1. Read Painting Materials, Preparing Project, Masking, Painting Project, Combing, and Sealing Project, page 73.

2. Mask off areas that will not be combed.

3. Prepare unmasked areas for painting. Paint unmasked areas brown.

4. Mix equal parts glazing medium and tan paint. Brush glaze mixture over base coat on top of chest; drag comb through wet glaze. Repeat for sides and drawers of chest, choosing different combing patterns for each side of chest.

5. Apply sealer to chest.

# old-fashioned floral dresser

Using floral fabric to match your room decor, cut out flower clusters and apply to drawer fronts with spray adhesive.

**You will need** a wooden dresser; matte tan acrylic latex wall paint; green, brown, and taupe acrylic paints; glazing medium; paintbrushes; 2"w painter's masking tape; yardstick; electric sander or sanding block with medium-grit sandpaper; floral print fabric; spray adhesive; sealer; and any additional supplies from Step 1.

1. Read Painting Materials, Preparing Project, Masking, Painting Project, Antiquing, Distressing, Striping, and Sealing Project, page 73.

2. Prepare dresser for painting. Paint dresser with two coats of tan wall paint.

Continued on pg. 42

# 7-drawer marbleized chest

impart regal splendor to a tall chest with our simple marbling technique. Just apply paint with a sponge, blend with a mop brush, and create veins with a feather.

**You will need** a wooden chest; ³/₄"w plywood cut to fit bottom of chest (optional); four legs and brackets (optional); matte cream acrylic latex wall paint; dark brown, brown, light brown, tan, white, and metallic gold acrylic paints; glazing medium; natural sponge; mop brush; paintbrushes; feather; primer; sealer; and any additional supplies from Step 1.

1. Read Painting Materials, Preparing Project, Masking, Painting Project, Painting Basics, Marbling, and Sealing Project, page 73.

2. To add legs to chest, nail plywood to bottom of chest. Mark desired placement of legs on plywood; attach brackets. Attach legs to brackets.

3. Prepare chest for painting. Paint chest using cream wall paint.

4. To create diamonds, measure length of one drawer and divide by two. Use a pencil to mark this measurement lightly at top and bottom of drawer. Measure width, divide by two, and mark sides. Lightly draw lines to connect pencil marks, forming a diamond. Repeat on each drawer.

5. Trace around diamond shape on one drawer; cut out. Use pattern to add diamonds to sides of chest.

6. Mask off just outside diamond edges. Basecoat inside each diamond with dark brown; let dry.

7. Mix equal parts glazing medium with brown, light brown, and tan paints.

Continued on pg. 42

# decoupaged rooster chest

**U**se narrow masking tape to help paint the plaid design on this little chest; then decoupage the rooster panels from wallpaper.

**You will need** a wooden chest; black, off-white, and red acrylic paints; crackle medium; #1 and #4 script liner brushes; paintbrushes; $3/4$"w painter's masking tape; wallpaper rooster panels; decoupage glue; primer; sealer; and any additional supplies from Step 1.

1. Read Painting Materials, Preparing Project, Masking, Painting Project, Painting Basics, Crackling, Striping, and Sealing Project, page 73.

Continued on pg. 43

25

# distressed dresser

*rub a candle over areas where you want the contrasting undercoat to show; then you can easily sand off spots of your new top coat for a distressed look.*

**You will need** a wooden dresser, desired paint or stain for underlying color (optional), matte white acrylic latex wall paint, white votive candle, wide household paintbrush, electric sander or sanding block with medium-grit sandpaper, wood trim for drawer, wood glue, sealer, and any additional supplies from Step 1.

1. Read Painting Materials, Preparing Project, Painting Project, Staining Project, Distressing, and Sealing Project, page 73.

Continued on pg. 43

# sponge-painted floral dresser

**turn a small wardrobe into a designer dresser with simple sponge-painting and a section of picket fencing.**

**You will need** a wooden wardrobe; matte white acrylic latex wall paint; white, blue, dark pink, pink, light pink, dark green, green, light green, periwinkle, yellow, pale yellow, yellowish white, plum, purple, and lavender acrylic paints; glazing medium; liner brush; paintbrushes; 1"w and 1¹/₂"w painter's masking tape; natural sponge; compressed sponges; slats from a roll of outdoor garden fence; saw; household cement; sanding block with medium-grit sandpaper; round wooden finials for feet; primer; sealer; and any additional supplies from Step 1.

1. Read Painting Materials, Preparing Project, Masking, Painting Project, Transferring Patterns, Painting Basics, Sponging, Striping, and Sealing Project, page 73.

Continued on pg. 43

27

# faux stained-glass wine rack

**C**ustomize a plain glass tabletop with our easy technique simulating stained glass. Just outline the design with dimensional paint and fill in with transparent glass paint.

**You will need** a wine rack with removable glass top; rose red, magenta, purple, blue, leaf green, kelly green, and clear transparent glass paints; charcoal gray dimensional paint (our project used three bottles); kraft paper; transparent tape; glass cleaner; lint-free paper towels; cotton swabs; and any additional supplies from Step 1.

1. Read Transferring Patterns, page 75.

Continued on pg. 44

# art deco gossip bench

αdd style to an old telephone desk with classic marbling, border paper, and a ritzy seat cover.

**You will need** a wooden gossip bench with removable seat; black, dark green, green, light green, yellow green, white, antique gold, metallic gold, and metallic copper acrylic paints; antique gold spray paint; glazing medium; natural sponge; mop brush; paintbrushes; primer; sealer; feather; five wooden napkin rings; wood glue; wallpaper border; fabric for seat; batting; staple gun; and any additional supplies from Step 1.

1. Read Painting Materials, Preparing Project, Masking, Painting Project, Painting Basics, Marbling, Sponging, Striping, Sealing Project, and Covering a Seat, page 73.

Continued on pg. 44

# picturesque writing desk

*Photocopy some pretty postcards to decoupage an antiqued desk painted with writing tools from yesteryear.*

**You will need** a wooden writing desk; matte white acrylic latex wall paint; burnt umber oil paint; burnt umber, red violet, white, blue, green, olive green, metallic gold, brown, light green, and black acrylic paints; toothbrush; small liner brush; #4 fan brush; paintbrushes; color copies of antique postcards; decoupage glue; primer; sealer; and any additional supplies from Step 1.

1. Read Painting Materials, Preparing to Paint, Painting Project, Transferring Patterns, Painting Basics, Antiquing, and Sealing Project, page 73.

Continued on pg. 44

# faux-tile tray table

transform a wooden tray with decoupaged pears and a faux-tile paint finish.

**You will need** wooden tray table(s); brown, tan, light tan, rust, and antique gold acrylic paints; off-white and tan acrylic latex wall paints; maple stain; 2"w angle paintbrush; paintbrushes; natural sponge; pear motif wallpaper border; Aleene's™ "Tacky" glue; soft cloth; primer; sealer; and any additional supplies from Step 1.

1. Read Painting Materials, Preparing Project, Masking, Painting Project, Painting Basics, Antiquing, Sponging, and Sealing Project, page 73.

2. Prepare table for painting. Mask off a 2" border around top edge of table. Paint border and edges brown. Remove tape.

Continued on pg. 45

# americana nightstand

refinish a bookcase-style nightstand with a patriotic paint job. Sand the edges to reveal underlying color for a timeworn effect.

**You will need** a wooden nightstand; desired paint or stain for underlying color (optional); matte white acrylic latex wall paint; red, white, and blue acrylic paints; electric sander or sanding block with medium-grit sandpaper; stiff-bristled paintbrush; paintbrushes; sealer; and any additional supplies from Step 1.

1. Read Painting Materials, Preparing Project, Masking, Painting Project, Staining Project, Transferring Patterns, Distressing, and Sealing Project, page 73.

Continued on pg. 45

# simple strawberry stool

Y ou'll finish this project in a snap — just sponge-paint the leafy background and handpaint with strawberries and more leaves.

**You will need** a wooden stool; white, ecru, green, dark green, red, and brown acrylic paints; paintbrushes; natural sponge; black medium-point permanent marker; primer; sealer; and any additional supplies from Step 1.

1. Read Painting Materials, Preparing Project, Painting Project, Sponging, and Sealing Project, page 73.

2. Prepare stool for painting. Paint stool ecru.

3. Referring to photo for color placement, sponge paint dark green, then green on stool top, legs, and rungs.

Continued on pg. 46

33

# no-sew fabric bed accents

Soften a bed with padded panels of coordinating fabrics that you glue in place.

**You will need** a double bed with wooden headboard and footboard, desired paint or stain for underlying color (optional), matte white acrylic latex wall paint, paintbrushes, electric sander or sanding block with medium-grit sandpaper, sealer, butcher paper, mat boards, craft knife, cutting mat, $1/2$" thick loft batting, fabrics for padded shapes and welting, spray adhesive, Aleene's ™ "Tacky" glue, $5/8$"w paper-backed fusible web tape, $5/16$" cotton cord, hot glue, and any additional supplies from Step 1.

1. Read Painting Materials, Preparing Project, Painting Project, Staining Project, Distressing, and Sealing Project, page 73.

2. Remove the old paint or stain from bed, if desired. (For this technique, you will paint and sand parts of bed, allowing underlying color to show through. Therefore, you may wish to remove existing color, then paint or stain bed the color to show through top coat.)

3. Prepare bed to be painted. Paint bed with two coats of white wall paint.

Continued on pg. 46

34

# handpainted roses headboard

let the unique contours of your headboard guide you in placing this beribboned garland of lovely handpainted roses.

**You will need** a twin bed with wooden headboard; matte off-white acrylic latex wall paint; white, light green, green, dark green, light gray blue, gray blue, dark gray blue, purple, dark purple, and yellow acrylic paints; glazing medium; small and large flat brushes; stiff-bristled brush; small round brush; liner brush; paintbrushes; natural sponge; soft cotton cloth; primer; sealer; and any additional supplies from Step 1.

1. Read Painting Materials, Preparing Project, Painting Project, Painting Basics, Sponging, and Sealing Project, page 73.

2. Prepare headboard for painting. Paint headboard using off-white wall paint.

3. Placement of roses and ribbons will depend on the contours of your headboard. Refer to photo, page 47, and very lightly sponge light green behind areas where you will paint roses and large leaves.

Continued on pg. 47

# country tapestry bench

*Spray-paint through a layer of dry beans to give this folk-art bench the look of a hooked rug.*

**You will need** a wooden bench; white, ecru, very dark gray, dark gray, gray, blue, dark blue, red, gold, light green, green, dark green, taupe, gray, brown, and olive acrylic paints; gray spray paint; oak stain; paintbrushes; natural sponge; dry navy beans (a 1 lb. bag for each square foot of bench top); 2"w painter's masking tape; electric sander or sanding block with medium-grit sandpaper; primer; sealer; and any additional supplies from Step 1.

1. Read Painting Materials, Preparing Project, Masking, Painting Project, Transferring Patterns, Antiquing, Distressing, Sponging, and Sealing Project, page 73.

2. Prepare bench for painting. Paint legs and bench supports white. Mask off 2"w border around top edge of bench. Paint border and edge of bench top olive; remove tape.

3. Mask off center of bench top. Sponge bench top with very dark gray, dark gray, and gray; remove tape.

4. Transfer patterns, pages 71 and 72, to bench top. Referring to photo for color placement, paint patterns.

5. Paint irregular patchwork border along inner edge of olive border.

6. To form rim to contain beans, apply tape along edge of bench top with $^3/4$" extending above surface. Spread beans in a single layer over surface of bench top so beans are touching without gaps. Spray paint surface until beans are evenly covered. Let dry completely. Remove tape and beans.

7. Repaint bench top border from edge to patchwork using olive paint.

8. Antique legs and bench supports using oak stain. For an aged effect, sand along edges and high spots on antiqued areas.

9. Apply sealer to bench.

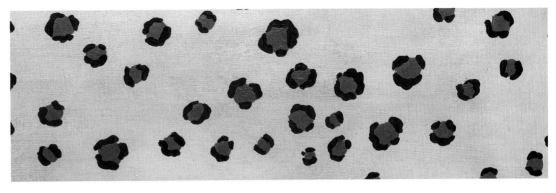

## leopard-print coffee table

4. Use maple stain to antique table. Apply a second coat of stain in random areas to create an irregular shading effect.

5. Wrap cloth around finger; dab into gold buffing cream and remove excess on paper towel. Rub over outside edges of tabletop.

6. Paint details on table supports metallic gold.

7. Apply sealer to table.

## technique sampler sofa table

3. Apply matte sealer to entire table. Prime drawers and unstained rectangle on tabletop.

4. Use a pencil to lightly mark twelve equal squares in the unstained rectangle. Each painting technique is applied to two squares. Mask off area just outside lines bordering squares you are working on. Remove tape as you finish.

5. For burled wood squares and drawers, basecoat with antique gold; let dry. Drybrush with metallic gold over basecoat. Mix equal parts glazing medium and burnt umber. Apply glaze mixture on one section at a time and sponge off.

6. For fossilized squares, basecoat with yellow green; let dry. Mix equal parts water and green paint. Apply thinned paint over base coat. While wet, squeeze drops of alcohol randomly onto surface. Wait a few seconds, then wipe off with cloth. Apply thinned paint and alcohol a second time; do not wipe off.

7. For malachite squares, basecoat with dark green; let dry. Mix equal parts glazing medium with green, light green, and yellow green paints. Apply each color with flat brush. Create malachite pattern with combing tool. Soften with mop brush.

8. For marbled squares, basecoat with dark green. Mix equal parts glazing medium with green, light green, and yellow green paints. Beginning with darkest color, sponge each mixture diagonally across square; blend using mop brush. Repeat marbling technique as needed.

For veins, mix one part white with two parts glazing medium. Use feather to apply glaze mixture, creating veins.

9. For tiger eye maple squares, basecoat with antique gold; let dry. Drybrush a small amount of metallic gold on base coat; let dry. Mix equal parts glazing medium and burnt umber. Apply glaze mixture to drybrushed area. While wet, press and lift folded plastic wrap across glazed area.

10. For tortoise shell squares, basecoat with metallic gold; let dry. Sponge lightly with antique gold. Sponge again with bronze. Mix equal parts water with burnt umber and black paints. Randomly sponge on each of these thinned paints. While wet, squeeze drops of alcohol randomly onto painted area; let dry.

11. For border lines, mix two parts glazing medium and one part black. Follow manufacturer's instructions to apply glaze mixture with striping tool.

12. Reapply matte sealer to entire table.

## refined accent table

3. Wrap cloth around finger. Dab into gold buffing cream; remove excess on paper towel. Rub over raised etchings and turnings on edge of tabletop, table support, legs, and leg supports.

4. Transfer photo patterns, pages 48 and 49, to tabletop and legs. Paint designs antique gold. Refer to pattern and use brown to shade designs. Paint gold highlights.

5. Add details to center flower using brown paint. Use metallic gold paint to outline designs and add details, following contours of tabletop.

6. Following manufacturer's instructions, apply crackle medium to table. Use antique gel to antique table.

7. Apply sealer to table.

## chinoiserie table

5. Side-load edges of islands, water, and reflections with metallic gold. Create a wash by mixing one part metallic gold paint with three parts water. Lightly apply wash to islands, water, and reflections.

6. Paint design areas according to photo. Shade with black. Use liner brush to add details with black and metallic silver.

7. Paint details on table legs metallic gold.

8. Apply sealer to table.

## work-of-art table

4. Transfer inside pattern lines on flowers and leaves. (Use side-load floats for all shading and highlighting.)

5. For purple flowers, use equal parts of light purple and purple for first shade color. Use purple for second shade color. Use violet for first highlight and off-white for second highlight. Paint centers blue. Add small light green tints to the edges of a few random petals. Paint centers with antique white dip dots and buds with antique white, light green, light purple, and blue dip dots.

6. For white flower, use antique white for first shade color. Use equal parts of antique white and light green for second shade color. Use off-white for first highlight and white for second highlight. Paint centers antique white. Add small light purple and blue tints to the edges of a few random petals. Paint centers with light green and green dip dots and buds with antique white, blue, light green, and green dip dots.

7. For light green leaves, shade with green. Paint dark green, then antique white veins.

8. For green leaves, shade with dark green. Paint dark green, then antique white veins.

9. For water drops, shade around outside of drops using dark green. Add white highlights to left side of drops. Use small liner brush to stroke a thin white line, then a dot on right side of drop.

10. Create each wash by mixing one part paint with two parts water. Wash light purple, blue, and light green on table edges and legs.

11. Transfer scrollwork photo patterns, pages 52 and 53, to tabletop and legs. Use metallic silver to paint scrollwork. Mix equal parts of metallic silver and black to outline scrollwork.

12. Apply sealer to table.

## painted lace accent table

2. Prepare tabletop for staining, if necessary. Stain tabletop dark oak. For this design, no primer is added to the area to be painted, allowing the wood grain to show through the painted lace doily.

3. Transfer lace doily photo pattern, page 54, to tabletop. Sand lightly inside the design with the grain of the wood. Wipe with tack cloth.

4. Create a wash by mixing one part white paint with two parts water. Brush wash on design in a circular motion with large flat brush. While wash is wet, lightly stroke dry mop brush over design to soften.

5. Use water to thin white paint to an ink-like consistency. Use liner brush to outline design and paint crisscross lines in lace border with thinned paint. Use small round brush to paint comma and eyebrow strokes. Paint graduated dip dots around edges of scallops; add dip dots along inner and outer circles.

6. Transfer outer edges of rose photo pattern, page 54, to tabletop. Basecoat rose and bud with pink. Basecoat stems and leaves with a mixture of two parts green and one part dark green.

7. Transfer inside pattern lines on rose. (Use side-load floats for all shading. Use drybrushing for all highlighting.)

8. For rose and bud, refer to photo pattern and use dark pink for first shade color and very dark pink for second shade color. Use pink for first highlight and light pink for second highlight.

9. For stems and leaves, use dark green for first shade color and very dark green for second shade color. Use green for first highlight and light green for veins and second highlight.

10. Apply sealer to table.

# fern-stamped coffee table

6. Take one frond from table and place it face-up on a sheet of paper. Roll brayer over frond until it is entirely covered with paint. Carefully pick up frond by stem and place it ink-side down on table. Place paper towel on top of frond and gently press frond to table. Remove paper towel and frond.

7. Refer to photo and repeat this process, reapplying paint to brayer and using new fronds, paper, and paper towels each time until desired coverage is complete. Be careful to avoid smudging the paint as you add new fern prints to the table.

8. Allow to dry for at least 24 hours.

9. Apply sealer to table.

# elegant-finish dining set

4. Mask around top edges of table using 1$\frac{1}{2}$"w tape. For rounded corners, apply tape diagonally across corners. Mark on tape with pencil to match the shape of the corner. Carefully cut tape with a craft knife, removing tape inside corner. Just inside the 1$\frac{1}{2}$"w tape, mask off with 2"w tape, rounding tape at the corners.

5. Mask alternate triangles on tabletop. For burled wood triangles and table pedestals, drybrush with metallic gold over base coat. Mix equal parts glazing medium and brown paint. Paint pedestals and one triangle at a time and sponge off. Let dry and remove tape. Mask remaining triangles and repeat burled wood technique, using dark brown instead of brown paint.

6. Use 2"w tape to mask just inside the 2"w tape on the table, rounding the corners. Remove outer 2"w tape. Center $\frac{1}{8}$"w tape on pencil lines that continue the triangles between taped areas.

7. For tortoise shell border, basecoat with metallic gold; let dry. Sponge lightly with antique gold. Sponge again with bronze. Mix equal parts water with burnt umber and black paints. Randomly sponge on each color thinned paint. While wet, squeeze drops of alcohol randomly onto painted area; let dry.

8. Mask off tortoise shell border and paint outer 1$\frac{1}{2}$"w border black.

9. Lightly redraw inner lines of medallion. Basecoat center circle and semi-circles black. Use side-load floats to paint black lines from edge to center of medallion.

10. Wrap cloth around finger; dab into gold buffing cream. Remove excess on paper towel. Rub over raised areas on table support and legs and along edge of tabletop.

11. Prepare chairs for painting.

12. Mask all areas except where burled wood technique is to be applied. Basecoat with antique gold. Drybrush with metallic gold over base coat. Mix equal parts glazing medium and brown paint. Paint a small section at a time and sponge off. Let dry and remove tape.

13. Mask around area where tortoise shell technique is to be applied. (Area to receive this technique must be lying flat.) Basecoat with metallic gold; let dry. Lightly sponge with antique gold. Sponge again with bronze. Mix equal parts water with burnt umber and black paints. Randomly sponge on each color thinned paint. While wet, squeeze drops of alcohol randomly onto painted area; let dry.

14. Mask as necessary and paint remainder of chair black.

15. Apply gold buffing cream to edges and raised areas.

16. Apply sealer to table and chairs.

17. Cover seats.

# fabulous '50s kitchen chairs

3. Mask off, then paint red bands on chair back spindles and seat supports. Paint red bands on the back side of chair back spindles.

4. Paint red wiggly lines on chair legs with #4 brush. Paint blue and yellow wiggly lines with #5/0 brush.

5. For cherry design, transfer cherry photo pattern, page 56, to front of two chair backs and back of two chair backs. Paint designs according to pattern. Follow contours of chair backs to paint thin red bands above and below cherry designs.

6. For plaid design, transfer plaid photo pattern, page 57, to remaining blank chair backs. Paint diagonal lines on chairs to imitate plaid pattern in your seat fabric or paint designs according to pattern, using #4 brush for red lines. Use #5/0 brush for blue and yellow lines.

7. Apply sealer to chairs.

8. Cover seats.

# kaleidoscope chair

3. Sponge paint dark green areas on chair back, legs, and supports. Referring to photo, paint yellow and orange free-form spots on sponged areas. Paint orange spots on white areas of legs.

4. Use black marker to detail yellow flower petals and orange spots.

5. Apply sealer to chair.

6. Cover seat.

# olde roses chair

3. Transfer outer edges of photo patterns, page 58, to chair back and seat supports, reversing corner rose pattern on upper left chair back and left seat support.

4. For bouquet and center roses, very lightly sponge light green behind roses and leaves.

5. For large leaves on bouquet, basecoat with green. Use a side-load float to shade with dark green. Add highlights and veins with white. For large leaves on center roses, basecoat with light green; shade with green. For large leaves on corner roses, basecoat with light green; add dark pink tints.

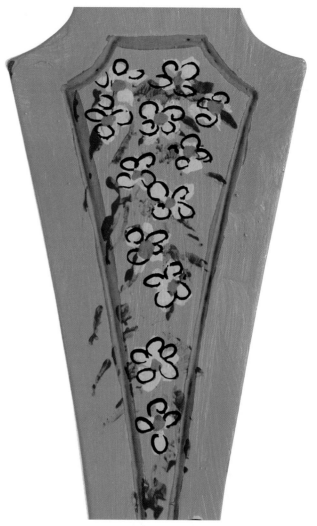

6. Basecoat all roses with dark pink. Follow stroke rose photo, page 77, to paint roses using flat brush double-loaded with dark pink and white. Add green tints to a few random petals. Add yellow dots to rose centers, using stiff-bristled brush and a stamping motion.

7. Basecoat blue flowers with white. Create a wash by mixing one part blue paint with two parts water. Apply wash to petals. Paint flower centers yellow; shade centers with gold.

8. For all small leaves, lightly double-load small flat brush with light green and dark pink. Use small, "S" strokes to paint leaves.

9. Use liner brush to add thin stems and tendrils with light green. Use small flat brush to add thick stems on bouquet with green; shade with dark pink.

10. Paint metallic gold detail lines, following contours of chair back.

11. Apply sealer to chair.

12. Cover seat.

# crackle-finish stenciled armoire

3. Follow manufacturer's instructions and use a roller to apply crackle medium to desired areas on armoire.

4. Using a soft brush and brushing from dry to wet areas, paint crackled areas with beige wall paint.

5. Paint inset panels on doors with cream wall paint.

6. Make stencils from photo patterns, pages 59 and 60. Flip stencils and arrange stencil elements on each inset as desired.

7. Mix two parts dark brown with one part cream wall paint. Stencil design according to patterns. Add highlights using metallic gold paint and cream wall paint.

8. Use metallic gold to drybrush dark brown areas that were not crackled.

9. Antique armoire with burnt umber.

10. Apply sealer to armoire.

# fanciful hutch

3. Refer to manufacturer's instructions to apply crackle medium to hutch on all areas except drawers, bases on top and bottom of hutch, trim on crown, inside trim on doors, and beaded paneling; let dry.

4. Use white wall paint to sponge crackled areas on top of hutch and brush crackled areas on bottom of hutch.

5. For vines, lightly pencil wavy lines; use #1 brush to paint lines navy blue. Use #10/0 brush to paint tendrils and stems of leaves navy blue.

6. For leaves on vines, mix equal parts navy blue and white acrylic paints. Mix equal parts of this mixture and water to create a wash. Apply wash to leaves using round brush. Outline leaves with navy blue.

7. Paint dots along trim on crown with thinned paint mixture used for leaves on vines.

8. For leaves on drawers and garland on base, use comma strokes and light green paint. Add yellow highlights to leaves.

9. For flowers on drawers, mix equal parts of navy blue and white acrylic paint; basecoat flowers. While wet, highlight tips of flowers using small round brush double-loaded with navy blue and white.

10. For flowers on garland, mix equal parts of navy blue and white acrylic paint. Paint two eyebrow strokes to form each petal. Shade petals with navy blue. Paint centers with navy blue dip dots.

11. Paint trim edges and cross-hatching navy blue.

12. Transfer outer edges of pitcher, cup, saucer, and topiary from photo patterns, page 61, to doors. Basecoat pitcher, cups, and saucers white. For topiaries, use stipple brush to apply light green and dark green paint with a stamping motion.

13. Transfer inside pattern lines to pitcher, cups, and saucers. Use equal parts of light gray and white for first shade color and light gray for second shade color. Paint details, leaves, tendrils, and flowers navy blue. Use water to thin white paint to an ink-like consistency. Use thinned paint to add highlights to leaves and flowers.

14. Paint topiary stems using flat brush double-loaded with brown and white paint. Paint greenery at top of cups and pitcher by stippling first dark green, then green paint.

15. Make two ivy leaf stamps by cutting two sizes of ivy-shaped pieces from craft foam. Glue small pieces of craft foam to backs of leaves for handles.

16. Mix equal parts of green and white paint. Thin dark green, green, and green mixture with water to ink-like consistencies. Dip ivy shapes in paint, dab on palette, and stamp randomly on topiaries, alternating colors. Use #10/0 brush to paint dark green vines.

17. Apply sealer to hutch.

# nautical-poster cabinet

3. Remove doors and any knobs from cabinet. Arrange doors side by side on back of desired portion of poster. Draw around doors; cut poster along drawn lines.

4. Apply spray adhesive to back of poster pieces. Adhere poster pieces to doors; smooth with brayer. Reattach any knobs.

5. Paint trim along edges of cabinet top with dark blue; let dry. Create "rope" by painting white "S" strokes approximately 1/4" apart along center of painted trim.

6. Transfer compass photo pattern, page 62, to top of cabinet. Paint design according to pattern using equal parts of water and dark blue paint for the lighter blue areas, and dark blue for dark areas and outlines.

7. Mask off 2"w stripes on sides of cabinet. Paint every other stripe with dark blue paint.

8. Mix equal parts glazing medium and white paint. Apply glaze mixture to trim and sides of cabinet.

9. Apply sealer to cabinet.

## pie safe with embossed insets

2. Remove the old paint or stain from pie safe, if desired. (For this technique, you will paint and sand parts of pie safe, allowing underlying color to show through. Therefore, you may wish to remove existing color, then paint or stain pie safe the color to show through top coat.) Use wood glue to attach trim to drawers; let dry.

3. Prepare pie safe to be painted. Paint pie safe with two coats of antique white wall paint.

4. Sand along edges and corners of pie safe and drawers, removing some paint to allow underlying color to show through.

5. Apply sealer to pie safe.

6. Paint embossed wallpaper using rusty brown. Paint a second coat using antique white wall paint. Sand wallpaper lightly. Wipe with tack cloth. Apply sealer to wallpaper.

7. Cut painted wallpaper to fit door insets. Apply spray adhesive to wrong side of wallpaper; mount on cardboard and cement in place on pie safe.

8. Cut mat board to fit inside doors. Cut fabric pieces 2" larger than mat board on all sides. Cut paper-backed fusible web same size as fabric pieces. Follow manufacturer's instructions to fuse web to wrong side of fabric pieces; remove paper backing. Center mat boards on fabric pieces. Carefully fuse center of fabric pieces to boards. Fold fabric over edges of boards, clipping as needed; fuse fabric in place. Cement covered mat boards inside doors; tape in place until secure.

9. Apply wallpaper to shelves and inside back of pie safe.

## color-washed cabinet

5. Create a wash by mixing one part rose with two parts water. Apply wash to rosebuds; let dry.

6. Create a wash by mixing one part white with two parts water. Side-load brush with wash and add highlights to rosebuds.

7. Create a wash by mixing one part green with two parts water to paint leaves.

8. Paint stems green.

9. Create a wash by mixing one part blue with two parts water to paint ribbon; shade with blue.

10. Apply sealer to cabinet.

## old-fashioned floral dresser

3. Measuring from sides of chest, mark center of chest top at front and back. Measure and lightly mark 1$\frac{1}{4}$" from each side of center marks. This gives you a 2$\frac{1}{2}$"w center stripe.

4. Use 2"w tape strips to connect marks at front of dresser top to marks at back of dresser top, leaving center stripe unmasked. Measure 2$\frac{1}{2}$" from outer edges of tape for placement of next tape strips. Continue across dresser. Repeat this process to mark stripes on each drawer.

5. Paint unmasked stripes green. Remove tape.

6. Mix equal parts glazing medium with brown paint. Antique dresser with glaze mixture.

7. Sand along edges and corners of dresser and drawers, removing some of the paint to allow underlying color to show through.

8. Cut motifs from fabric. Apply spray adhesive to wrong side of motifs; smooth onto drawer fronts. Shade around motifs with taupe paint.

9. Apply sealer to dresser.

## 7-drawer marbleized chest

8. Beginning with darkest color, sponge each mixture diagonally across diamonds; blend using mop brush. Repeat marbling technique as needed.

9. For veins, mix one part white with two parts glazing medium. Use feather to apply glaze mixture, creating veins. Remove tape.

10. Outline diamonds with metallic gold.

11. Mask off and add geometric lines to sides and top of chest using metallic gold.

12. Apply sealer to chest.

# decoupaged rooster chest

2. Prepare chest for painting. Mask off rectangular area with curved corners on top of chest. Paint chest black. Paint drawers and masked area on top off-white.

3. Refer to manufacturer's instructions to apply crackle medium to sides of chest; let dry.

4. Brush red paint on crackled areas.

5. Mark center of chest top and drawers. Create vertical stripes of equal width using $^3/_4$"w tape. Leaving center stripe off-white, paint every other stripe red. Remove tape. Repeat to create horizontal stripes.

6. Draw a pencil line through center of each vertical and horizontal red stripe. Use #4 brush to paint every other pencil line black and remaining pencil lines off-white.

7. Draw a light pencil line through center of each horizontal and vertical off-white stripe. Use #1 brush to paint every other pencil line red and remaining pencil lines black.

8. Cut out rooster panels from wallpaper. Decoupage rooster panels to drawers.

9. Apply sealer to chest.

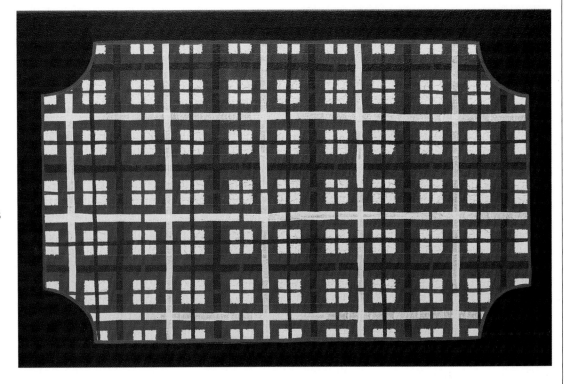

## distressed dresser

2. Remove the old paint or stain from dresser, if desired. (For this technique, you will apply wax and paint, then sand the dresser, allowing underlying color to show through. Therefore, you may wish to remove existing color, then paint or stain dresser the color to show through top coat.)

3. Rub candle over areas where underlying color is to show. Rub off excess wax shavings. Paint dresser white. Sand all surfaces, removing wax.

4. Glue trim to top drawer.

5. Apply sealer to dresser.

## sponge-painted floral dresser

2. Prepare wardrobe for painting. Cement finials to legs. Paint wardrobe using white wall paint.

3. Mask off vertical stripes on sides of wardrobe alternating 1"w and 1$^1/_2$"w strips of tape. Paint 1"w stripes yellow.

4. Referring to photo for color placement, paint drawers and door yellow. Paint edgings and trim periwinkle and blue. Paint leg details periwinkle and pink.

5. Mix equal parts glazing medium with white wall paint. Apply glaze mixture to door and drawer fronts.

6. Use natural sponge to sponge paint sky blue and grass green on door.

7. Transfer pattern pieces, page 68, to compressed sponges; cut out. Sponge paint white and blue checkerboard patterns around drawers.

8. Follow numbered photo pattern, page 68, to sponge shaded flowers and leaves on drawers, using pinks and greens.

9. Use pink to sponge random spots to bottom of wardrobe.

10. Follow numbered photo pattern to sponge paint garden scene on door. Use liner brush to add details to door.

11. Cut fence to fit door. Hold one slat against door and mark desired position of rails. Paint rails white. Sand slats lightly to give them a worn appearance; cement to door.

12. Apply sealer to wardrobe.

## faux stained-glass wine rack

2. Cut kraft paper same size as glass top.

3. Make several photocopies of patterns, page 69. Cut around shapes and arrange on kraft paper, leaving room for border design; tape in place.

4. Place clean glass top on kraft paper pattern. (Glass must be dry and lint-free.)

5. Use dimensional paint to outline designs and add border. (Work from left to right if you are right-handed or from right to left if you are left-handed to keep your arm from smudging wet paint. Wipe away any mistakes with cotton swab and reapply paint.) Draw connecting lines between patterns for stained-glass effect; let dry overnight.

6. Apply paints directly from bottles to areas outlined with dimensional paint. Fill in leaves with leaf green and kelly green, using tips of bottles to mix colors on glass as you paint. Paint grapes with magenta, rose red, purple, and blue, using solid colors in some grapes and mixing colors in others. Paint border with desired colors.

7. Fill in empty areas around grape clusters and leaves with clear paint.

8. Allow paint to cure for several days. You may wish to place a second piece of glass on top of stained-glass piece for protection.

## art deco gossip bench

2. Prepare bench for painting. Paint bench black. Basecoat area to be marbled with dark green; let dry.

3. Mix equal parts glazing medium with green, light green, and yellow green.

4. Beginning with darkest color, sponge each mixture diagonally across bench top; blend using mop brush. Repeat marbling technique as needed.

5. Mix one part white with two parts glazing medium. Use feather to apply glaze mixture, creating veins.

6. Mask off narrow vertical stripes around body of bench. Sponge stripes using antique gold, metallic gold, and metallic copper.

7. Spray paint napkin rings antique gold. Glue one ring to bottom of each leg.

8. Apply sealer to bench.

9. Follow manufacturer's instructions to apply wallpaper border around body of bench.

10. Cover seat.

## picturesque writing desk

2. Prepare desk for painting. Paint desk with white wall paint. Antique desk using burnt umber oil paint.

3. Dip toothbrush into burnt umber acrylic paint. Hold toothbrush next to desk surface; run thumb over toothbrush bristles to spatter-paint desk.

4. Transfer photo patterns, pages 65 - 67, to desk top.

5. For violets, outline top two petals with red violet. Float across bottom of petals with brush side-loaded with red violet. Float across top of petals with brush side-loaded with equal parts of red violet and white acrylic paints.

Outline bottom three petals with blue. Float across bottom of petals with brush side-loaded with blue. Float across top of petals with brush side-loaded with equal parts of blue and white acrylic paints.

6. For leaves and stems, float around leaf and down center with brush side-loaded with green. Shade with olive green. Use small liner brush to paint stems and tendrils green.

7. For glasses, basecoat with metallic gold; shade with burnt umber acrylic paint. Paint shadows cast by the glasses with brown. Paint highlights on rims and lenses with white acrylic paint.

8. For pen, basecoat tip with metallic gold. Shade with burnt umber acrylic paint. Add highlights with white acrylic paint. For metal band, basecoat with green; shade with olive green. Paint light green highlights.

9. For feather, paint quill brown. Paint highlights with white acrylic paint. Mix equal parts brown and white acrylic paints; thin slightly with water. Work thinned paint into #4 fan brush; tap handle of brush on table to separate bristles. Stroke feather area. Use brown to stroke feather area lightly and randomly; repeat with white acrylic paint.

10. Basecoat inkwell with green. Drybrush areas to be highlighted on lid and lip of inkwell with equal parts of green and light green. Shade under rim and inside top with olive green. Paint ink black. Highlight ink with equal parts of white and black acrylic paints. Paint rim with metallic gold. Outline rim and screws with burnt umber acrylic paint.

11. Decoupage color copies of postcards to table.

12. Lightly shade around all objects with burnt umber acrylic paint.

13. Apply sealer to desk.

# faux-tile tray table

**3.** Within brown border, mask off bottom $^1/_2$" of side edges of table and $^1/_8$"w strip along inner edges of border. Sponge paint border tan, then light tan, allowing a little of the brown border to show through. Randomly sponge paint a small amount of rust on border. Remove tape. Paint thin brown lines every 2" on border to resemble tiles.

**4.** Mask off center of table along inner edge of border. Place a small amount of white and tan wall paints on palette. Dip angle brush in both colors. Create textured center of table by stroking with an "X" motion. Remove tape.

**5.** Cut pear shapes from wallpaper border; glue to center of table.

**6.** Antique center of table, using cloth to rub maple stain into the paint texture.

**7.** Mask off a $^1/_4$"w border $^3/_8$" from tile border. Paint border with antique gold.

**8.** Apply several coats of sealer to table for durability.

# americana nightstand

**2.** Remove the old paint or stain from nightstand, if desired. (For this technique, you will paint and sand parts of nightstand, allowing underlying color to show through. Therefore, you may wish to remove existing color, then paint or stain nightstand the color to show through top coat.)

**3.** Prepare nightstand to be painted. Paint with two coats of white wall paint.

**4.** Sand high spots and edges, removing some paint to allow underlying color to show through.

**5.** Adjusting for the size of your nightstand top, determine the number and width of your stripes, allowing for an even number of red stripes. Mask off areas to remain white; paint unmasked areas red. Remove tape. Use stiff-bristled brush to feather hard edges of stripes.

**6.** Refer to photo, page 32, and mask off a rectangle in upper left corner of nightstand top. Paint rectangle blue using two coats of paint. Remove tape. Use stiff-bristled brush to feather hard edges of rectangle.

**7.** Transfer pattern, page 70, to center of rectangle. Paint star white.

**8.** Paint front of drawers blue.

**9.** Sand high spots and edges once again to create an aged effect.

**10.** Apply sealer to nightstand.

## simple strawberry stool

4. Paint strawberries where desired using red. While wet, paint highlights and seeds using white.

5. Paint strawberry caps using dark green. Referring to photo, paint free-form leaves with dark green and green paints.

6. Paint stems brown.

7. Use black marker to outline and detail berries, leaves, and stems.

8. Apply sealer to stool.

## no-sew fabric bed accents

4. Sand along edges and corners of bed, removing some paint to allow underlying color to show through.

5. Apply sealer to bed.

6. For padded shapes, use butcher paper to make patterns, following contours of headboard and footboard; cut out.

7. Draw around patterns on mat board and batting; cut out. Cut fabric pieces 3/4" larger than patterns on all sides.

8. Apply spray adhesive to one side of mat board. Adhere batting to mat board. Wrap fabric around mat board, clip curves, and glue edges to back of

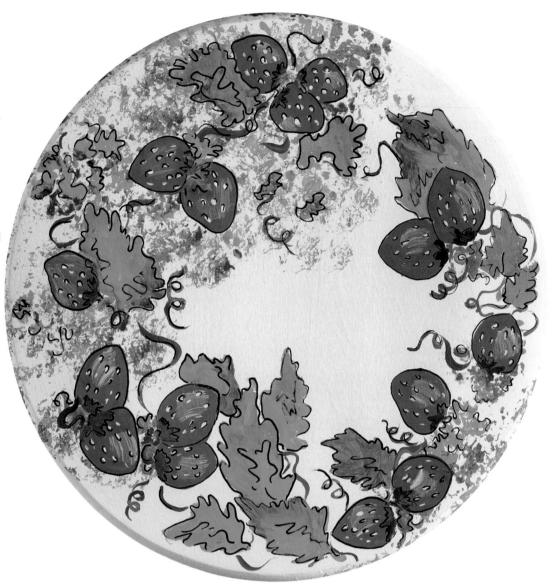

board. Repeat for remaining padded shapes.

9. For welting, measure around edges of padded shape; add 2". Cut a 2" wide bias strip of fabric the determined measurement, piecing fabric as necessary. (To piece two strips together, fuse web tape to right side of each fabric strip along one short edge. Remove paper backing. Matching right sides, fuse taped edges together; press seam allowance to one side.) Fuse web tape to wrong

side of fabric strip along both long edges; remove paper backing. Cut a length of cord same length as fabric strip. Center cord on wrong side of fabric strip. Matching long edges, fold strip over cord; fuse.

10. Beginning and ending 2" from ends of welting, glue welting seam allowance to back of padded shape, clipping at corners. Leaving a 1" overlap, trim welting. Pull apart 2" of

fused edges from trimmed end of welting, pulling bias strip away from cord. Trim cord only so that cord ends meet. Fold trimmed end of bias strip 1/2" to wrong side. Wrap folded edge around remaining end of welting; glue in place. Repeat for remaining padded shapes.

11. Hot glue padded shapes to headboard and footboard.

# handpainted roses headboard

4. For large leaves, basecoat with green. Use a side-load float to shade with dark green. Paint white highlights and veins.

5. Paint ribbons with large flat brush double-loaded with gray blue and light gray blue. Shade folds of ribbon with a side-load float of dark gray blue.

6. Basecoat all roses with dark gray blue. Follow stroke rose photo, page 77, to paint roses using large flat brush double-loaded with purple and white. Add purple dots to rose centers, using stiff-bristled brush and a stamping motion. Repeat, adding yellow dots.

7. Paint random white dip dots on leaves and rose petals.

8. For each small flower, paint five stroke petals using small round brush loaded with dark purple and dipped in white. Paint yellow dot at each flower center.

9. For small filler leaves, load small flat brush with green and use small, "S" strokes to paint leaves. Large filler leaves are lightly basecoated with green.

10. Use liner brush to paint stems and tendrils with light green.

11. Paint top edge of headboard gray blue.

12. Refer to photo, page 35, to paint bedposts dark gray blue, green, purple, and gray blue. Mix equal parts glazing medium and off-white wall paint; apply glaze mixture to bedposts. While wet, lightly wipe with cloth.

13. Apply sealer to headboard.

# refined accent table
(page 7)

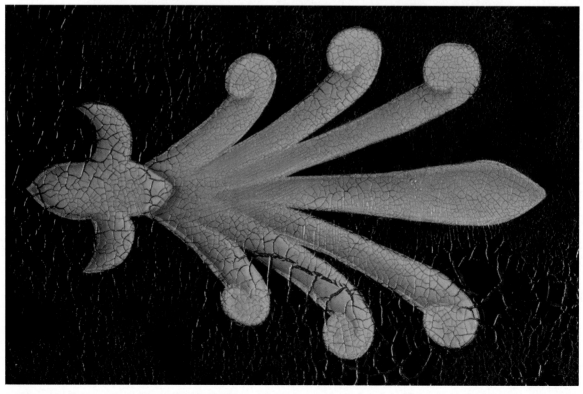

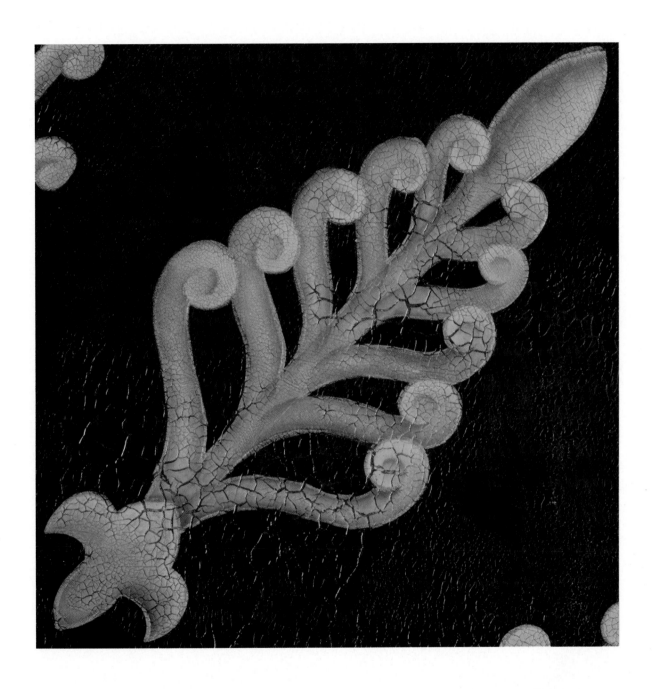

# chinoiserie table
## (page 8)

# work-of-art table
## (page 9)

# painted lace accent table
## (page 10)

# elegant-finish dining set
## (page 12)

# fabulous '50s kitchen chairs
## (page 13)

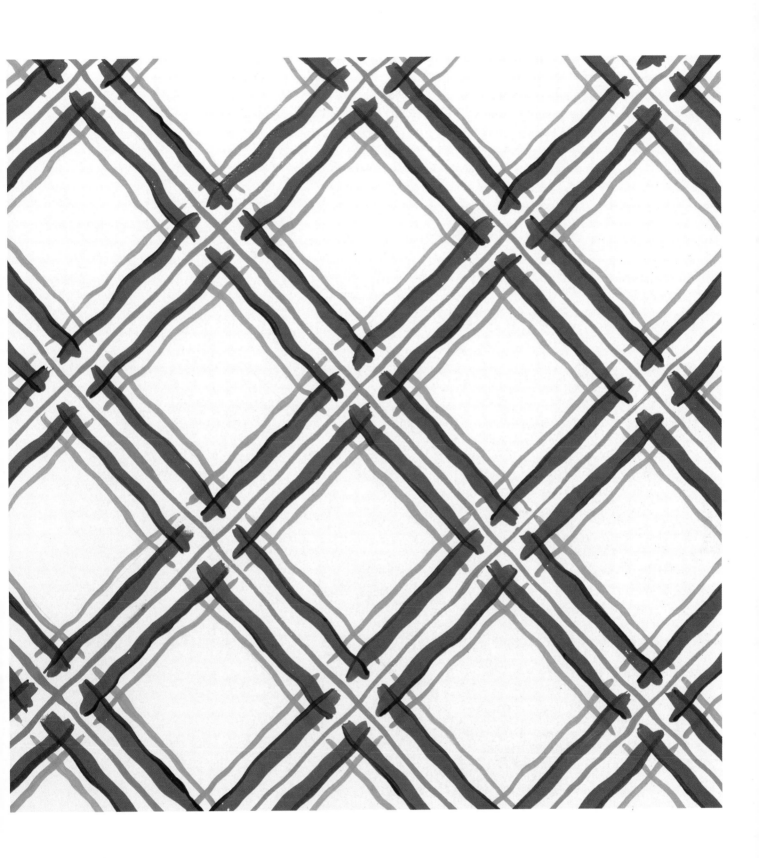

# olde roses chair
## (page 15)

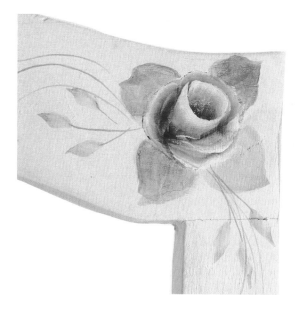

# crackle-finish stenciled armoire
## (page 16)

# crackle-finish stenciled armoire
## (continued)

# fanciful hutch
## (page 17)

# nautical-poster cabinet
## (page 18)

# color-washed cabinet
## (page 20)

# sunny gingham-look cupboard
## (page 21)

# picturesque writing desk
## (page 30)

# sponge-painted floral dresser
## (page 27)

# faux stained-glass wine rack
## (page 28)

# americana nightstand
## (page 32)

# country tapestry bench
(page 36)

# country tapestry bench
## (continued)

# GENERAL INSTRUCTIONS

## Painting Materials

### Primers

Primers seal the wood, preventing the wood grain from rising or any underlying paint colors from showing. Don't prime projects you are distressing if you want the original paint, stain, or grain to show through. If you're painting unfinished wood, use a stainblocking primer to keep the knotholes from bleeding through the paint. For previously painted or stained surfaces, use a sandable spray primer or a brush-on primer; fill and sand any imperfections that appear after priming. Reapply primer to sanded areas.

### Paints

For large pieces of furniture, we recommend that you basecoat using a water-based acrylic latex wall paint. Water-based acrylic craft paint is less durable, but works well on smaller pieces and for painting details. Because oil-based paint has to be cleaned with mineral spirits and is more toxic than water-based paint, we only recommend using oil paint for projects that require a thicker paint with a slow drying time.

### Glazing Medium

Glazing medium mixed with paint gives the paint a longer drying time and makes the paint translucent, allowing undercoats to show through. You can purchase glazing medium separately and mix it with your paint, or you can buy it already pre-mixed or have the store tint it for you.

### Stains

Stains allow the natural grain of the wood to show through. Follow manufacturer's instructions to apply a water-based stain, first testing the color on a part of your piece that won't show.

### Sealers

Sealers protect the finish on your painted or stained projects. We recommend that you use a water-based sealer that is designed to be used on furniture. Water-based varnish will give you a thick seal. Varnish is sandable, and you may apply several coats to your project, sanding lightly with steel wool between each coat. Polyurethane sealers are available in matte, satin, and gloss finishes and can be brushed or sprayed on, according to your preference.

### Painter's Masking Tape

We recommend using bright blue low-tack painter's masking tape on your projects. Regular masking tape will become sticky after about eight hours and may pull the paint up as you remove the tape from your project. Painter's tape isn't as sticky, and can remain on your piece of furniture up to three or four days before removal.

### Sandpaper

Properly sanding your piece is essential for smooth finished surfaces. Liquid sandpaper followed by steel wool works well to remove old sealer from projects with detailed carving. You can also use fine- and medium-grit sandpaper to prepare your furniture. An electric sander is useful for distressing wood after painting. Large sheets of sandpaper may be purchased in packages and then cut to fit your sander. Sanding sponges are useful when sanding curved surfaces.

### Tack Cloth

A tack cloth is a sticky piece of fabric used to remove fine dust after sanding.

### Graphite Transfer Paper

When tracing a pattern onto your project, use white graphite paper on a dark surface or dark graphite paper on a light surface. A stylus or a pen works better than a pencil when transferring fine lines.

### Foam Rollers and Brushes

Disposable foam brushes and rollers are often used to apply the primer. It's easy to apply the base coat on a large piece of furniture with a roller; however, it will leave a slight texture on the piece. For a smoother surface, a household brush works best.

### Household Paintbrushes

Use household brushes to basecoat small furniture pieces. To clean water-based paint from your brush, rinse thoroughly with cool water. Use mineral spirits to clean oil-based paint.

### Artist's Paintbrushes

Use artist's brushes to paint details. To clean, pour mild detergent or paintbrush cleaner in palm of hand. Stroke bristles through cleaner, pushing metal band into palm. Squeeze bristles between thumb and fingers. Rinse well under cool running water, washing paint from metal band and bristles. Blot with a paper towel; lay flat to dry.

## Sponges

Natural sponges work well when applying paint in a random manner. Compressed sponges are useful when you want to sponge paint definite shapes onto your project. The desired shape can be drawn or traced on the flat sponge and easily cut out.

## Combing Tools

Combing tools are available with teeth of varying widths. You can also make your own tool by using a craft knife to cut out notches from a rubber squeegee or sturdy piece of cardboard.

## Striping Tool

Follow manufacturer's instructions and use a striping tool to apply a thin, even line of paint. This tool is very useful when you want to make precise, straight lines.

# Preparing Project

**For safety's sake**, carefully follow all manufacturers' instructions and warnings when using any cleaning, stripping, painting, staining, or finishing product. For children's furniture, use non-toxic paints, stains, primers, and sealers that are recommended for that purpose.

**You may need** household cleaner, oil soap, sponges, soft cloths, old paintbrush, toothbrush, paint/varnish stripper, wood putty, putty knife, paint scraper, wire brush, assorted grit or gauge sandpaper or steel wool, tack cloth, and items for repairing furniture (hammer, screwdriver, drill, nails, screws, clamps, wood glue), primer, and paintbrushes.

Before you paint or stain, your goal is to have the furniture piece in working condition, clean, and ready to accept paint or stain.

1. Remove seat or drawers from your piece of furniture.

2. Make repairs and remove hardware. Number the pieces as you remove them to help you put them back in the original place.

3. Fill holes and small imperfections with wood putty. Knock off any peeling or chipping paint with a paint scraper, wire brush, or putty knife.

4. If you wish to keep the original paint or stain on your furniture piece, use a non-abrasive cleaner such as oil soap to clean the piece. For unfinished wood or to remove existing paint or stain, sand carved surfaces with steel wool, liquid sandpaper, or a sanding sponge and flat surfaces with medium-grit sandpaper. Always sand with the grain of the wood. If your furniture piece has many layers of paint or a lumpy surface, you may wish to follow manufacturer's instructions and use a paint stripper to get down to the original wood.

5. The type of finish currently on your piece determines the final preparations.

**Unfinished wood to be stained** — Sand again with fine-grit sandpaper. Wipe with tack cloth.

**Unfinished wood to be painted** — Sand again with fine-grit sandpaper. Wipe with tack cloth. Apply a stainblocking primer. Lightly sand, then wipe with tack cloth.

**Painted or stained surfaces to be painted** — Sand again with fine-grit sandpaper. Wipe with tack cloth. Apply a sandable spray primer or a brush-on primer.

## Masking

**You will need** painter's masking tape in appropriate width(s), a ruler or yardstick, and a pencil.

To mask off straight edges, apply masking tape along the edge of an area that you don't wish to paint. Apply paint to surface; let dry and remove tape.

To mask off curved areas, apply tape to surface where you want to paint the curve. Draw the curve freehand or use a compass to draw a portion of a circle on tape. Use a craft knife to gently cut tape along curved line. Remove curved part of tape from the area you are about to paint. Apply paint to surface; let dry and remove remainder of tape.

# Painting Project

**You may need** painter's masking tape, kraft paper, paint, and paintbrushes.

1. In most cases, you will need to paint the entire surface a single background color before you add decorative details or finishes.

2. Using masking tape and kraft paper as needed, mask off any area that you don't wish to paint.

3. Apply paint using a paintbrush, a roller if you desire texture in your base coat, or use spray paint. The paint may require more than one coat for even coverage.

4. Once the background color is dry, follow individual project instructions for finishing. Practice on poster board or on a part of your project that won't show before painting details or applying decorative finishes to your furniture piece.

## Staining Project

**You may need** painter's masking tape, kraft paper, water-based stain, and paintbrushes.

1. Using masking tape and kraft paper as needed, mask off any area that you don't wish to stain.

2. Test the color of the stain on a part of your project that won't show. Apply stain following manufacturer's instructions.

3. Once the stain is dry, follow individual project instructions for finishing.

## Transferring Patterns

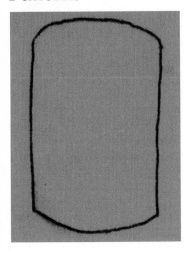

**You will need** tracing paper; graphite paper; and a stylus, pen, or dull pencil.

1. To reduce or enlarge patterns on a photocopier to fit your furniture piece, first decide how large you would like the pattern to be. A good rule is to leave 1/2" to 1" of space around the edges to frame your design.

2. Divide the desired height or width (whichever is larger) by the height or width of the pattern. Multiply this number by 100%. Photocopy the pattern at this percentage.

Example: You want the pattern to be 8" high on your project. It is 4" high on the pattern page. 8/4=2 and 2x100%=200% You will copy the pattern at 200%.

3. Trace photocopied pattern onto tracing paper. Position tracing paper on surface; slide graphite paper between tracing paper and surface; tape in place with removable tape. Use a stylus, pen, or dull pencil to lightly trace over the outside lines of the pattern. Use an art gum eraser on any smudges or lines that are too dark. Basecoat; let dry. Reposition pattern and trace all detail lines.

## Painting Basics

**You will need** to practice these decorative painting basics to achieve the desired results.

### Basecoating

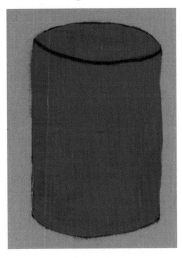

Dip flat paintbrush in water; dip in paint. Apply thin coat of paint to surface, smoothing with wet paint to prevent any ridges; let dry. Lightly sand with inside of brown paper sack and wipe with tack cloth. Repeat for one or two more coats. Reapply detail lines.

### Shading

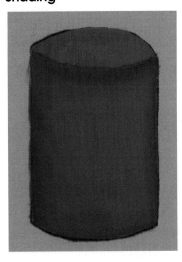

One way to create depth in painting is to shade recessed areas and any areas that are furthest from the imagined light source. Shade using side-load floats or drybrushing as indicated in project instructions.

### Highlighting

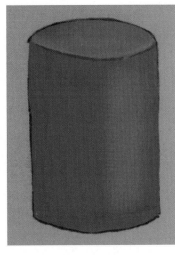

Achieve dimension in painting by highlighting areas that are in the forefront or are closest to the imagined light source. Use side-load floats or drybrushing to add highlights according to project instructions.

### Tints

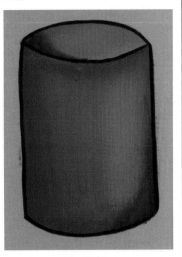

Tints tie the colors of the design together. Use a side-load float and a small amount of paint to apply contrasting colors to areas that you want to emphasize, such as tinting a leaf with a bit of pink from a nearby rose.

The image shows various brushes and their stroke results, labeled: Side-load Float, Comma Stroke, Eyebrow Strokes, Drybrushing, Lining, Long Strokes, Dip Dots, Feathers and Foliage, "S" Stroke, "C" Stroke, Double-loading

## Side-load Float

Dip flat or angle paintbrush (shown) in water; blot on paper towel. Pick up paint on one corner of the brush. Use short strokes to gently blend on your palette, keeping the clean side of your brush free from paint. Turn the brush over and lightly blend on the palette. Paint should be on one edge of the brush, gradually fading to clear water on the other edge.

Dip a clean flat paintbrush in water; blot on paper towel. Lightly dampen the surface to be floated so your float will glide on smoothly. Hold the loaded brush with the color on the left, parallel to surface. Stroke lightly, pulling the brush toward you. Blend any imperfections with a mop brush. If additional color is desired, let surface dry completely before floating again.

## Comma Stroke

Dip round brush in water; blot on paper towel. Pick up small amount of paint on lower half of bristles. Hold brush at 45° angle to surface. Touch tip of paintbrush to surface, allowing brush hairs to spread out. Pull paintbrush toward you, lifting brush gradually to form the tail of the stroke.

## Eyebrow Strokes

Begin in the same way as the comma stroke, then pull round brush to the right or left as you create the tail of the stroke.

## Drybrushing

Do NOT dip brush in water. Dip stipple brush or old round paintbrush (shown) in paint; wipe most of the paint off onto a dry paper towel. Lightly rub the brush in a circular motion, starting in the center of the area to receive color. Decrease pressure on the brush as you move outward. Repeat as needed.

## Lining

For most lining, use #18/0 or #10/0 liner brush (shown). Thin paint to an ink-like consistency. Dip brush in water; blot on paper towel. Load brush by placing bristles in paint and dragging away from puddle to get a pointed tip. Hold brush perpendicular to surface, about 1" above metal band. Place tip on surface and pull brush toward you. Pull from your elbow, not from your wrist. When paint begins skipping, reload brush and begin again, backing up a little from where you ended to keep line the same width.

## Long Strokes

To create long strokes, dip script liner brush in paint. Pull brush toward you, looking about 1" ahead of the tip of the brush as you pull. Script liners hold more paint than liner brushes and long lines can be completed without interruption.

## Dip Dots

Dip the handle end of paintbrush in paint. Touch end of paintbrush to surface. To make dots the same size, dip end of paintbrush into paint each time. To make graduated sizes, place largest dot first, then continue dotting surface without reloading end of brush with paint.

## Feathers and Foliage

Work paint thinned with water into fan brush. Tap brush handle on table to separate bristles. Stroke lightly to create feathers or foliage.

## "S" Stroke

Dip angle or flat paintbrush (shown) in paint. Touch tip to surface, pulling brush to the left. Pull brush toward you while applying pressure. When stroke is desired length, raise brush up to the tip and pull to the left.

## "C" Stroke

Dip angle or flat paintbrush (shown) in paint. Touch tip to surface, pulling brush to the left. Pull brush toward you while applying pressure. When stroke is desired length, raise brush up to the tip and pull brush to the right.

## Double-loading

Dip flat paintbrush in water; blot on paper towel. Pick up paint on one corner of the brush. Pick up the second color on the other corner. Use short strokes to gently blend on one area of your palette to keep the colors clean. Turn your brush over and blend the other side. When loaded properly, each true color should be on opposite edges of the brush, with the colors gradually blending in the middle.

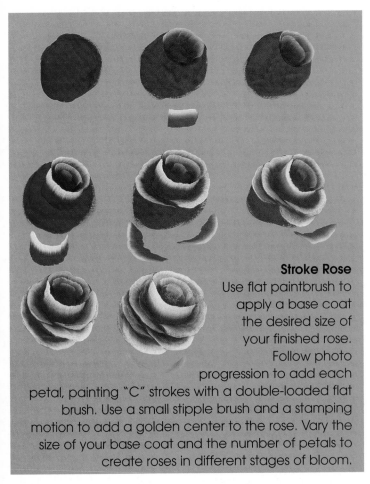

**Stroke Rose**
Use flat paintbrush to apply a base coat the desired size of your finished rose. Follow photo progression to add each petal, painting "C" strokes with a double-loaded flat brush. Use a small stipple brush and a stamping motion to add a golden center to the rose. Vary the size of your base coat and the number of petals to create roses in different stages of bloom.

## Antiquing

**You will need** appropriate stain, paint, or antiquing gel; blending and glazing medium if using oil paint; foam brushes; soft cloth; and paper towels.

Antiquing gives wood an aged appearance and softens the colors on your project. The stain, paint, or gel can be applied to bare wood, over paint, or over a clear sealer. To achieve a timeworn effect, the antiquing should be darker around the edges of the project and lighter toward the middle. Test on an inconspicuous area to assure desired results.

To antique using pre-mixed stain, antiquing gel, or thinned acrylic paint, apply with a foam brush, paper towel, or soft cloth. Work in one small area at a time; wipe immediately with a clean, soft cloth or paper towel to remove excess color. Let dry. Repeat as desired for darker color.

To antique using oil paint, wrap cloth around finger; dab into a small amount of blending and glazing medium and then pick up a very small amount of paint. Work in a circular motion beginning in corners and around edges. Use a clean, soft cloth to blend into the antiqued area. If an area becomes too dark, rub a little glazing medium into area to lighten.

## Burled Wood

**You will need** a small natural sponge, glazing medium, paint, and paintbrushes.

Drybrush a small amount of paint in a circular motion randomly over base coat; let dry. Stroke paint mixed with glazing medium over surface. While paint is wet, dip sponge in water and squeeze to remove excess water. Press sponge on surface, twist, and lift to create a small circle. Repeat randomly, overlapping circles at times and pressing harder in some areas to remove more paint.

## Combing

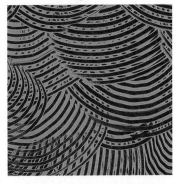

**You will need** glazing medium, combing tool, paints in contrasting colors to allow combing pattern to show, and flat paintbrush.

Mix glazing medium with paint that contrasts with base coat. Use flat brush to apply glaze mixture over dry base coat. Drag the combing tool through the wet glaze mixture, picking up the glaze and allowing the base coat to show through. Wipe comb off each time you lift it from the surface. Form different patterns by turning the comb different ways. Use your combing tool to create fans, wavy stripes, cross hatching, and malachite patterns.

# Crackling

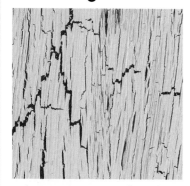

**You will need** crackle medium, paint, paintbrushes, roller (optional), and natural sponge (optional). If you're working on a large project, you may wish to purchase a quart-size container of crackle medium available at home improvement stores.

1. For long, wide cracks, basecoat with a semi-gloss or gloss finish paint. For fine cracks, basecoat with a matte or satin finish paint.

2. Follow manufacturer's instructions to apply crackle medium with a brush or roller. If you don't wish to apply a top coat of paint, choose a crackle medium that doesn't require a top coat, such as Jo Sonja's® Crackle Medium.

3. For a project with a top coat of paint, apply paint with a flat brush to achieve long, wide cracks. For fine cracks, use a natural sponge to apply paint. Since crackling process begins immediately, do not brush back over the top coat. After reloading brush, paint the next stroke by brushing toward the area where you last applied paint, instead of away from it.

# Distressing

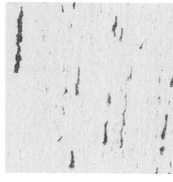

**You will need** a project that has been painted or stained (this color will show through the distressed top coat), electric sander, medium-grit sandpaper, paint, and paintbrush.

To create an aged effect, apply one or two coats of paint to project; let dry. Sand high spots and edges, removing some of the paint so undercoat of paint or stain shows through.

Another method allows more of the undercoat to show through. Rub a white votive candle over areas that you want to look distressed, applying a thick coat of wax so that paint can be easily removed from those areas. Lightly rub all surfaces with the palm of your hand to remove excess wax shavings. Apply paint to project with a wide brush (you don't have to be concerned about neatness); let dry. Sand all surfaces. Waxed areas will sand down to the original finish. Change sandpaper often.

# Fossilizing

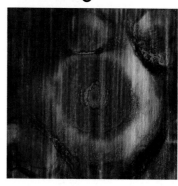

**You will need** isopropyl alcohol (other types of alcohol won't work), eyedropper, paint, paintbrush, and soft cloth.

Fill eyedropper with alcohol. Brush paint thinned with water over dry base coat. While wet, gently squeeze alcohol drops over painted area. Let alcohol react with paint a few seconds, then wipe off with cloth. Apply thinned paint and drops of alcohol a second time; do not wipe off.

# Malachite

**You will need** glazing medium, combing tool, paints in contrasting colors to allow combing pattern to show, mop brush, and flat paintbrush.

Mix glazing medium with paints that contrast with base coat. Use flat brush to randomly apply each glaze mixture on dry base coat. Swirl combing tool through wet glaze mixture in tight half-circles to create malachite pattern. Use a light stamping motion with mop brush to soften texture.

# Marbling

**You will need** glazing medium, natural sponge, paint, mop brush, and large feather.

Dip damp sponge into darkest paint color; blot on paper towel. Dab over base coat diagonally, leaving some base coat showing through. Turn sponge slightly after you lift it to create a random pattern. Working quickly so paint doesn't dry, repeat with medium and then light paint colors. Lightly blend with a mop brush.

Use a feather to create veins. Drag feather through paint, then wiggle and flip feather as you drag it diagonally across marbled area. Add smaller branches off the main veins.

## Sponging

**You will need** natural sponge or compressed sponge, paper towels or sheets of paper, and paint.

For random sponging, lightly dip damp natural sponge into paint. Blot sponge on paper towel to remove excess paint. Dab sponge onto base coat; lift sponge straight up, then turn slightly to create a random pattern. Reload sponge as needed. Continue sponging as desired, allowing some of the base coat to show through.

For shaded sponge shapes, cut desired shape from compressed sponge. Wet sponge to expand. Place light, medium, and dark paint colors on a palette or a paper plate. Saturate sponge with medium color. Dip one side of shape in dark color; tap on sheet of paper to blend, then press sponge on surface. Blend light and medium colors in this same way, sponging where desired. Reload color often to keep colors intense and shapes well-defined.

## Stenciling

**You will need** sheet of stencil plastic, black fine-point permanent pen, cutting mat or several layers of newspaper, craft knife, fine-grit sandpaper, tape or stencil adhesive, paint, and stencil brushes.

1. Cut a piece of stencil plastic 1" larger on all sides than photo pattern. Center plastic piece over pattern; use pen to trace outlines of pattern.

2. Place plastic piece on cutting mat; use craft knife to cut out stencil along pen lines. Lightly sand cut edges to smooth any rough spots.

3. Use stencil adhesive or tape to hold stencil in place while stenciling.

4. Use a clean, dry stencil brush for each color of paint. Use a paper plate or a dish for your paint so that only the flat part of the brush receives the paint. Dip tips of bristles in paint; remove excess paint on a paper towel. Brush should be almost dry to produce a good design.

5. Begin at edge of cutout area and apply paint in a stamping or a circular motion. Shade design by applying more paint around edge than in center. Carefully remove stencil.

6. If you repeat the pattern several times, paint may build up in the fine cuts of your stencil. Clean the stencil as needed with soap and water; dry thoroughly.

7. To stencil designs in reverse, clean stencil and dry thoroughly. Turn stencil over and repeat process.

## Striping

**You will need** appropriate size(s) of painter's masking tape, yardstick, pencil, paint, and paintbrushes.

The easiest way to stripe is to choose the width(s) of your stripes from among the available sizes of painter's masking tape. Use a pencil to mark the center top and bottom of the surface you wish to stripe. Center the tape between these marks. Apply second piece of tape along either side of center tape strip, butting edges together without overlapping. (To achieve uniform stripes, use only one size of tape.) Continue working out to the sides of the surface, alternating your tape sizes, if desired. Remove the tape from the stripes you wish to paint. Apply paint; let dry. Remove tape.

If you want stripes to be a width that's unavailable in painter's tape, choose the width of your center stripe. Mark the center of your surface and measure half the desired stripe width toward the right. Mark this measurement at top and bottom of surface; lightly draw a line between marks. Repeat, measuring to the left from center. Continue measuring and marking stripes. Use painter's tape to mask off along edges of the stripes that won't be painted. Apply paint; let dry. Remove tape.

## Tiger Eye Maple

**You will need** glazing medium, plastic wrap, paint, and paintbrushes.

Drybrush a small amount of paint from side to side on base coat. Stroke paint mixed with glazing medium sideways over surface, leaving paint streaky. While wet, fold plastic wrap into a 3/4" wide strip. Lay strip from top to bottom of glazed area; press lightly, lift, and repeat across entire glazed area. Use a fresh piece of plastic wrap as needed.

## Tortoise Shell

**You will need** isopropyl alcohol (other types of alcohol won't work), eyedropper, natural sponge, paint, and paintbrush.

Basecoat area to be painted with your lightest color; let dry. Lightly sponge next two shades over base coat; let dry. Fill eyedropper with alcohol. Randomly sponge on the thinned paint colors. While wet, gently squeeze alcohol drops over painted area; let dry.

## Sealing Project

Protect the finish on your project with a water-based varnish or polyurethane sealer. Apply several coats to pieces that will receive everyday practical use, such as a tabletop. Allow each coat of sealer to dry thoroughly after each application.

## Covering a Seat

**You will need** fabric to cover seat, batting, and staple gun.

1. Remove seat from chair. Draw around seat on wrong side of fabric. Cut out fabric 4" outside drawn line. Cut batting same size as seat. (You may need to cut several layers of batting for desired thickness of seat.) Layer batting, then seat on wrong side of fabric.

2. Pulling fabric taut, staple the center of opposite fabric edges to bottom of seat. Repeat with the other two edges. Work from the center to the corners, stretching the fabric evenly and rotating the seat after each staple.

3. For corners, fold sides first and then the top and bottom edges, carefully tucking edges so they won't be visible from the top of the seat.

4. Staple fabric to corners of seat bottom.

5. Reattach seat to chair.

## Production Team

**Designers:** Patti Sowers and Dani Martin
**Contributing Designers:** Linda Ansel (Handpainted Roses Headboard, page 35, and Olde Roses Chair, page 15) and Cynthia Lewis (Simple Strawberry Stool, page 33, and Kaleidoscope Chair, page 14)
**Staff Photographer:** Russ Ganser
**Photography Stylists:** Sondra Daniel, Karen Hall, Tiffany Huffman, Elizabeth Lackey, and Janna Laughlin
**Production Artist:** Dana Vaughn
**Technical Writer:** Laura Siar Holyfield
**Editorial Writer:** Steven M. Cooper